21st Century
Basic Skills
Library

KIDS CAN MAKE MANNERS COUNT
PUT YOUR STUFF AWAY!

by Katie Marsico

Cherry Lake Publishing • Ann Arbor, Michigan

Published in the United States of America
by Cherry Lake Publishing
Ann Arbor, Michigan
www.cherrylakepublishing.com

Content Adviser: Tonia Bock, PhD, Associate Professor of Psychology,
St. Thomas University, St. Paul, Minnesota

Photo Credits: Cover and pages 1, 4, 6, 8, 14, 16, 18, 20, ©Denise
Mondloch; page 10, ©iStockphoto.com/nicolesy; page 12,
©Phase4Photography/Shutterstock, Inc.

Library of Congress Cataloging-in-Publication Data
Marsico, Katie, 1980–
  Put your stuff away! / by Katie Marsico.
     p. cm.—(21st century basic skills library) (Kids can make manners
count)
  Includes bibliographical references and index.
  ISBN 978-1-61080-439-4 (lib. bdg.) — ISBN 978-1-61080-526-1 (e-book) —
ISBN 978-1-61080-613-8 (pbk.)
1. Orderliness—Juvenile literature. 2. Etiquette for children and
teenagers—Juvenile literature. I. Title.
  BJ1533.O73M37 2012
  395.1'22—dc23   2012001713

Cherry Lake Publishing would like to acknowledge
the work of The Partnership for 21st Century Skills.
Please visit www.21stcenturyskills.org for more information.

Printed in the United States of America
Corporate Graphics Inc.
July 2012
CLFA11

TABLE OF CONTENTS

A Messy Artist

Molly loved doing projects in art class.

She liked using crayons and markers to make pictures.

Molly also drew with chalk and colored pencils.

Molly did not think cleaning up was much fun.

She left huge messes in the classroom. Art **supplies** were sometimes lost or ruined.

This **bothered** her teacher Ms. Williams.

Making Manners Work

Molly enjoyed art class.

Yet she hated spending time cleaning up.

Ms. Williams talked to Molly. She told Molly why it was important to clean up.

Ms. Williams said that putting things away showed good **manners.**

It was **rude** to leave messes for other people to clean up.

Molly said that she put her stuff away at home.

She picked her toys up off the floor.

Molly also helped her parents clear the table after dinner.

Always Cleaning Up

Ms. Williams asked Molly to clean up in art class.

This made it easier for everyone to use the art supplies.

Molly started putting away art supplies when she was done.

Molly returned crayons, pencils, and chalk to their boxes. Other people could easily find them later.

She put caps back on all the markers. This stopped the markers from drying out.

Soon Molly never forgot to clean up in class.

This helped everyone in art class work more easily.

There was less of a mess when the bell rang.

Ms. Williams was happy with Molly's good manners. She really liked Molly's artwork, too!

Find Out More

BOOK

Huget, Jennifer LaRue, and Edward Koren (illustrator). *How to Clean Your Room in 10 Easy Steps.* New York: Schwartz & Wade Books, 2010.

WEB SITE

U.S. Department of Health and Human Services—Building Blocks: Manners Quiz

www.bblocks.samhsa.gov/family/activities/quizzes/manners.aspx

Take a fun online quiz to test how much you know about manners!

Glossary

bothered (BAH-thurd) hurt or upset

manners (MA-nurz) behavior that is kind and polite

rude (ROOD) having bad manners

supplies (suh-PLYZ) items someone uses to complete a project

Home and School Connection

Use this list of words from the book to help your child become a better reader. Word games and writing activities can help beginning readers reinforce literacy skills.

a	clear	hated	messy	rang	there
after	colored	helped	Molly	really	things
all	could	her	Molly's	returned	think
also	crayons	home	more	rude	this
always	did	huge	Ms.	ruined	time
and	dinner	important	much	said	to
art	doing	in	never	she	told
artist	done	it	not	showed	too
artwork	drew	later	of	sometimes	toys
asked	drying	leave	off	spending	up
at	easier	left	on	soon	use
away	easily	less	or	started	using
back	enjoyed	liked	other	stopped	was
bell	everyone	lost	out	stuff	were
bothered	find	loved	parents	supplies	with
boxes	floor	made	pencils	table	when
caps	for	make	people	talked	why
chalk	forgot	making	picked	teacher	Williams
class	from	manners	pictures	that	with
classroom	fun	markers	projects	the	work
clean	good	mess	put	their	yet
cleaning	happy	messes	putting	them	

23

Index

About the Author

Katie Marsico is an author of children's and young-adult reference books. She lives outside of Chicago, Illinois, with her husband and children.